Cold, Colder, Coldest

Animals That Adapt to Cold Weather

by Michael Dahl ~ illustrated by Brian Jensen

PICTURE WINDOW BOOKS
Minneapolis, Minnesota

Thanks to our advisers for their expertise, research, and advice:

Dr. James F. Hare, Associate Professor of Zoology
University of Manitoba
Winnipeg, Manitoba

Susan Kesselring, M.A., Literacy Educator
Rosemount-Apple Valley-Eagan (Minnesota) School District

Editorial Director: Carol Jones
Managing Editor: Catherine Neitge
Creative Director: Keith Griffin
Editor: Christianne Jones
Story Consultant: Terry Flaherty
Designer: Nathan Gassman
Production Artist: Angela Kilmer
Page Production: Picture Window Books
The illustrations in this book were created with pastels.

Picture Window Books
5115 Excelsior Boulevard, Suite 232
Minneapolis, MN 55416
877-845-8392
www.picturewindowbooks.com

Printed in the United States of America.

Library of Congress Cataloging-in-Publication Data
Dahl, Michael.
Cold, colder, coldest : animals that adapt to cold weather /
written by Michael Dahl ; illustrated by Brian Jensen.
p. cm. — (Animal extremes)
Includes bibliographical references and index.
ISBN 1-4048-1014-5 (hardcover)
1. Cold adaptation—Juvenile literature. I. Jensen, Brian, ill.
II. Title.

QH543.2.D34 2006
591.4'2—dc22   2005003731

Animals live everywhere. They fly over the highest mountains and swim in the deepest oceans. They run over the hottest deserts and dive into the coldest waters.

Some animals live in extremely cold climates. Watch the temperatures on the thermometer dip to chilling lows as you turn each page.

Zzzz-zzzzz!

4

An Arctic bumblebee flies above the frosty tundra. It survives 40° F.

°F

140

120

100

80

60

40
40° Fahrenheit
4° Celsius

20

0

-20

-40

-60

-80

°C

60

50

40

30

20

10

0

-10

-20

-30

-40

-50

-60

Can any animal exist in a colder climate?

Yes! The Alaska blackfish can!
It survives minus 4° F as it darts
through Alaskan waters.

Can any animal exist in a colder climate?

°F

140

120

100

80

60

40

20

0

-4° Fahrenheit
-20° Celsius

-20

-40

-60

-80

°C

60

50

40

30

20

10

0

-10

-20

-30

-40

-50

-60

Yes! The Antarctic skua can! It survives minus 12° F. It steals another bird's egg near the coast of Antarctica.

Can any animal exist in a colder climate?

°F

°C

80

30

20

60

10

40

0

20

-10

0

-20

-12° Fahrenheit
-24° Celsius

-20

-30

-40

-40

-50

-60

-80

-60

Yes! The ptarmigan can!
It walks out of its snow
burrow in Greenland.
It survives minus 29° F.

Can any animal exist in a colder climate?

-29° Fahrenheit
-34° Celsius

Yes! The polar bear can! It survives minus 34° F as it walks over the ice-covered waters of northern Canada.

Can any animal exist
in a colder climate?

°F
140 —
120 —
100 —
80 —
60 —
40 —
20 —
0 —
-20 —
-34° Fahrenheit
-37° Celsius
-40 —
-60 —
-80 —

°C
— 60
— 50
— 40
— 30
— 20
— 10
— 0
— -10
— -20
— -30
— -40
— -50
— -60

Yes! The musk ox can! It huddles with other oxen to stay warm in the minus 40° F winds of the Arctic plains.

Can any animal exist in a colder climate?

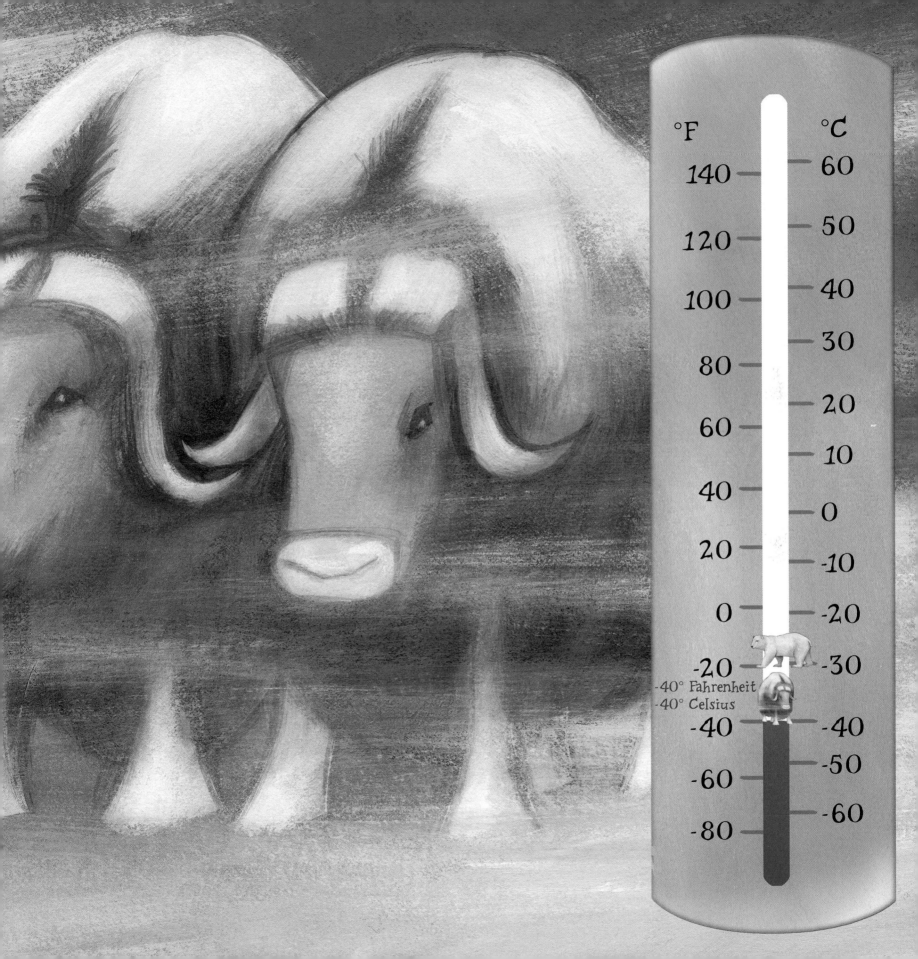

°F

140 —
120 —
100 —
80 —
60 —
40 —
20 —
0 —
-20 —
-40° Fahrenheit
-40° Celsius
-40 —
-60 —
-80 —

°C

60
50
40
30
20
10
0
-10
-20
-30
-40
-50
-60

Yes! The emperor penguin can! It survives minus 70° F as it waddles around in the Antarctica snow.

Can any animal exist in a colder climate?

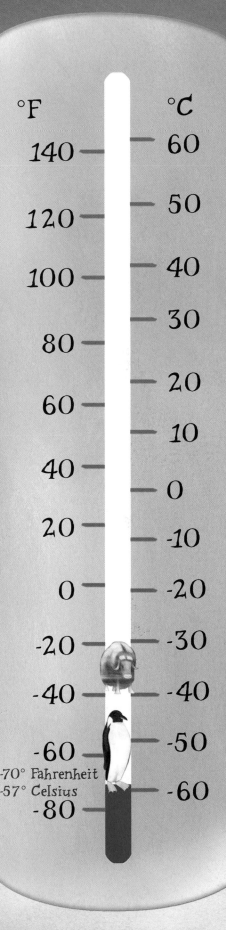

°F   °C
140 — — 60
       — 50
120 —
100 — — 40
       — 30
80 —
       — 20
60 —
       — 10
40 —
       — 0
20 —
       — -10
0 —
       — -20
-20 — — -30
-40 — — -40
       — -50
-60 —
-70° Fahrenheit
-57° Celsius
-80 — — -60

Yes! The Siberian husky can!
It stands guard on the cold
Siberian snow. It survives
minus 75° F.

Can any animal exist
in a colder climate?

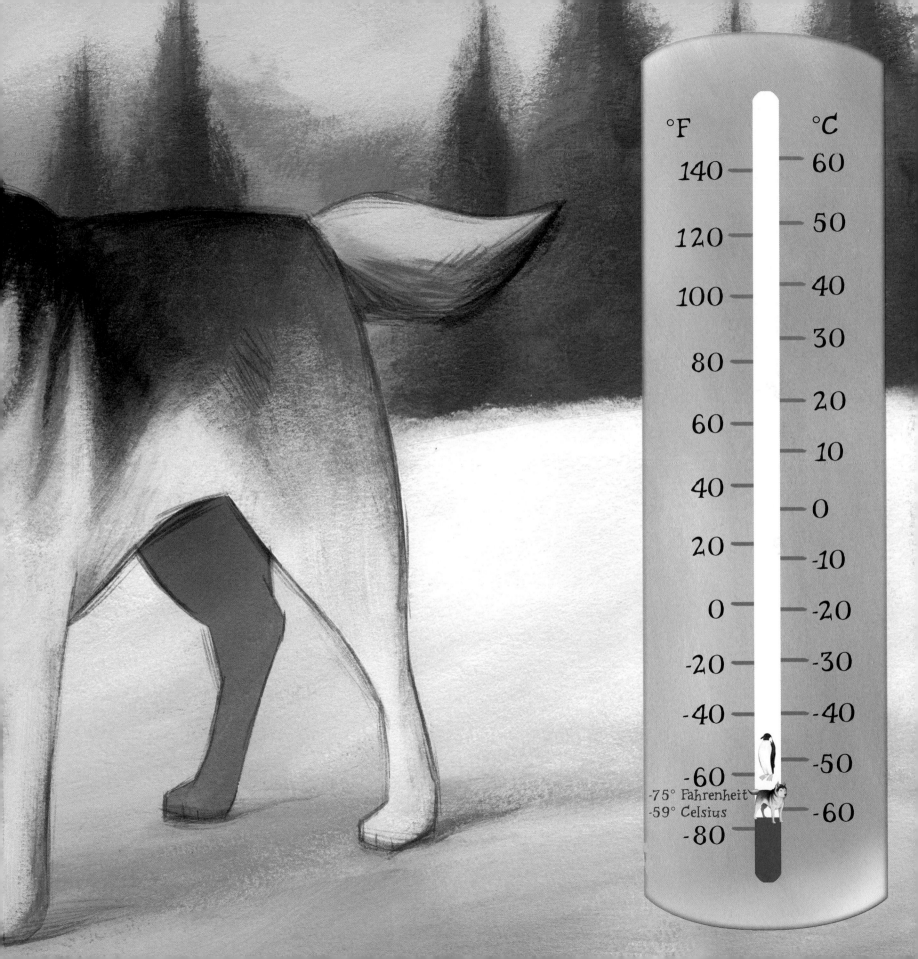

°F

140 —

120 —

100 —

80 —

60 —

40 —

20 —

0 —

-20 —

-40 —

-60 —

-80 —

°C

— 60

— 50

— 40

— 30

— 20

— 10

— 0

— -10

— -20

— -30

— -40

— -50

— -60

-75° Fahrenheit
-59° Celsius

Perhaps. Who knows what could exist in colder climates?

Extreme Fun

Arctic bumblebees shiver to generate heat. Their thick hairs trap the heat to keep them warm.

Arctic bumblebee

The Alaska blackfish lives in colder water than any other fish on Earth.

Alaska blackfish

Antarctic skuas are also called brown skuas. They are very aggressive birds.

Antarctic skua

The ptarmigan turns white in winter. Its white coloring helps it blend in with the snowy surroundings.

ptarmigan

A thick layer of blubber keeps the polar bear warm while swimming in cold water.

polar bear

Facts

The musk ox has broad hooves that spread out flat. These flat feet help keep the ox from sinking into the deep snow.

musk ox

Thick fat and two layers of thick feathers keep the emperor penguin warm in freezing weather.

emperor penguin

Siberian huskies were brought to Alaska from Siberia in 1909. They were used as sled dogs because of their great speed and endurance.

Siberian husky

Glossary

aggressive—ready to attack

blubber—a layer of fat

burrow—a hole or tunnel in the ground made by an animal, usually for its home

endurance—the ability to keep going when things are difficult

fierce—very strong or violent

hooves—hard coverings on the feet of some animals

huddle—to crowd tightly together in a group

plains—flat, grassy land with only a few trees

survive—to stay alive

thermometer—a tool for measuring temperature

tundra—an area of flat or rolling plains with no trees

To Learn More

At the Library

Berger, Valerie. *What do Animals do in Winter? How Animals Survive the Cold.* Nashville: Ideals Children's Books, 1995.

Butterfield, Moira. *Animals in Cold Places.* Austin, Texas: Raintree Steck-Vaughn, 2000.

Glassman, Jackie. *Amazing Arctic Animals.* New York: Grosset & Dunlap, 2002.

On the Web

FactHound offers a safe, fun way to find Web sites related to this book. All of the sites on FactHound have been researched by our staff.
www.facthound.com

1. Visit the FactHound home page.

2. Enter a search word related to this book, or type in this special code: 1404810145

3. Click on the FETCH IT button.

Your trusty FactHound will fetch the best sites for you!

Index

Look for all of the books in the Animal Extremes series:

Cold, Colder, Coldest: *Animals That Adapt to Cold Weather*

Deep, Deeper, Deepest: *Animals That Go to Great Depths*

Fast, Faster, Fastest: *Animals That Move at Great Speeds*

High, Higher, Highest: *Animals That Go to Great Heights*

Hot, Hotter, Hottest: *Animals That Adapt to Great Heat*

Old, Older, Oldest: *Animals That Live Long Lives*